1st Grade Books For Boys Science Edition

Frog Life Cycle

SPEEDY PUBLISHING

The Egg

Frogs lay their
eggs in water
or wet places.

A floating clump
of eggs is called
frog spawn.

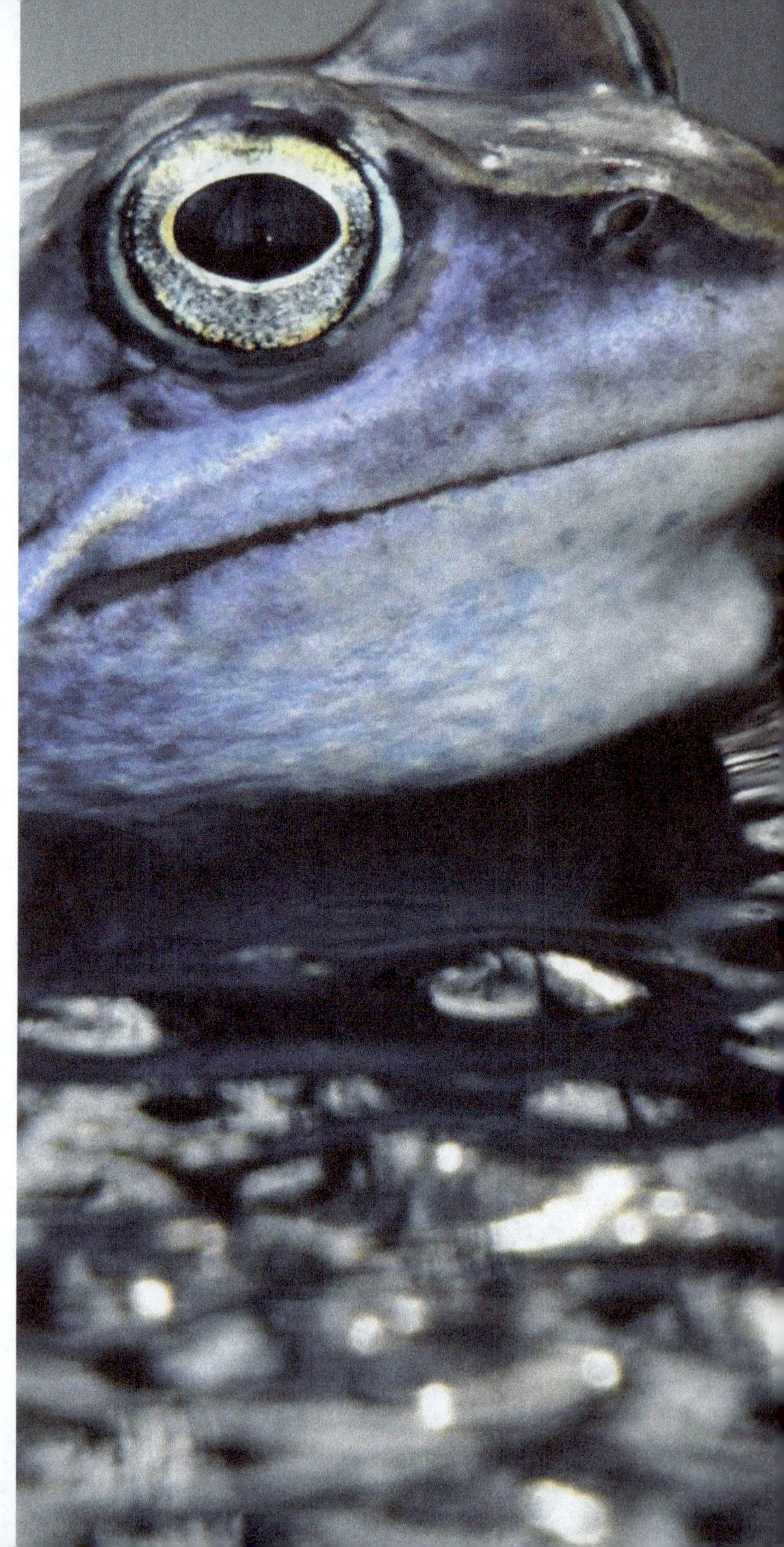

The Cell Splits

The single cell in the egg eventually splits into two.

From two they
split making
four cells,
and so on.
Eventually,
there are many
cells in the egg.

The
Embryo

The mass of
cells in the egg
come to form
an embryo.

Organs and gills begin to form, and in the meantime, the embryo lives off of its internal yolk.

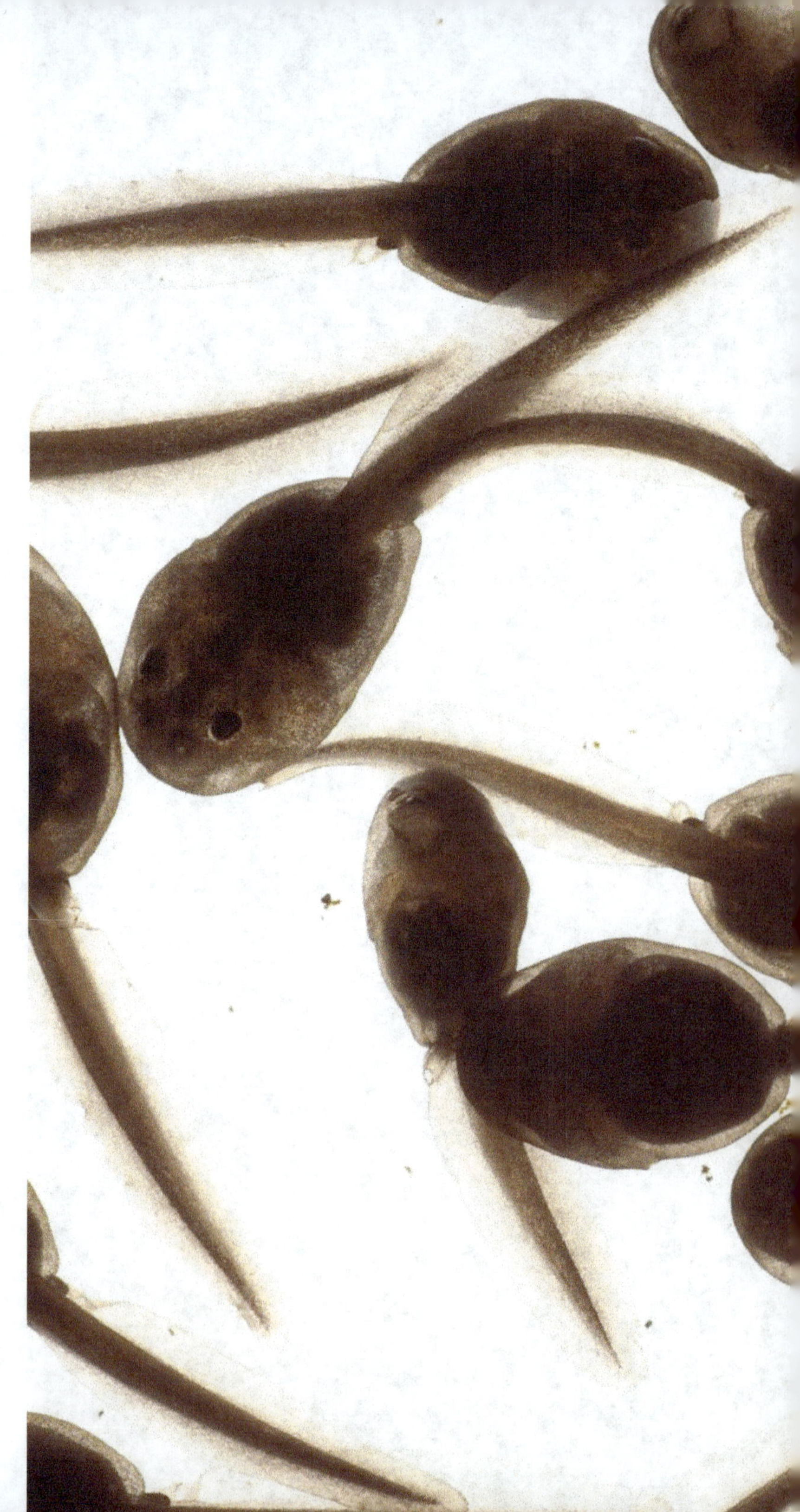

The
Tadpole

The tadpole has
a long tail, and
lives in the water.

It is extremely
vulnerable, and
must rely on
its camouflage
to protect it.

After about
five weeks, the
tadpole begins to
change. It starts
to grow hind
legs, which are
soon followed
with forelegs.

The Frog

Eleven weeks after the egg was laid, a fully developed frog with lungs, legs, and no tail emerges from the water

This frog will live
mostly on land,
with occasional
swims.

The tiny frogs begin
to eat insects and
worms. Eventually,
it will find a mate.

The female frog lays the eggs, the male fertilizes them, and **the whole process begins again**.

Visit
BABY PROFESSOR
EDUCATION KIDS
www.BabyProfessorBooks.com
to download Free Baby Professor eBooks
and view our catalog of new and exciting
Children's Books